Original title:
The Sea's Unspoken Words

Copyright © 2025 Creative Arts Management OÜ
All rights reserved.

Author: Natalia Harrington
ISBN HARDBACK: 978-1-80587-359-4
ISBN PAPERBACK: 978-1-80587-829-2

The Quietude of Ocean Sorrows

Waves whisper secrets, loud to the shore,
But seagulls squawk jokes, asking for more.
Crabs in their shells do a little dance,
While starfish just wish for a second chance.

The tide rolls in with a giggly sigh,
Jellyfish float by, waving goodbye.
Each splash has a punchline, the tide seems to tease,
As fishermen chuckle and young kids all freeze.

Unvoiced Dreams of Coastal Sands

Footprints drawn in soft, golden sand,
Shells tell the stories of life unplanned.
A crab takes a stroll, he trips on a rock,
While seagulls swoop down for a snack and a talk.

The ocean murmurs in a funny tone,
While the tide pulls back, it makes a groan.
Fish in their fins play peek-a-boo hail,
As mermaids giggle, sharing their tales.

Tidings from the Water's Edge

Splashing waves giggle as they race to the land,
Each droplet a jest, each ripple well-planned.
The sandcastles tumble under a wave's playful trick,
While dolphins swim circles, performing a flick.

A barnacle gives two snorts and a shout,
As seaweed dances, swirling about.
Seashells gossip like old ladies chat,
Claiming the biggest tide's just a rough spat.

Fables of a Moonlit Sea

Under the moon, the waves tap-tap-tap,
A fish with a hat is caught in a flap.
The ocean's deep laughter reflects on the tide,
As crabs throw a party, with shells dignified.

Starfish tell tales of their many lost shoes,
While dolphins play soccer with jelly-filled blues.
An octopus paints under the starlit array,
Making sea creatures giggle 'til break of the day.

Tide's Hidden Language

The waves giggle and swirl,
Tickling the shore with each twirl.
Shells gossip, oh what a sight,
As crabs dance, all filled with delight.

Seagulls squawk, with tales to tell,
About jellyfish who fell and fell.
Fish flash their scales, a cheeky grin,
While starfish snicker, 'Who's diving in?'

Echoes of the Deep

Bubbles burble, secrets in tow,
Octopus winks, 'You don't want to know!'
The clownfish chuckles as they play,
In their bright homes, they frolic all day.

Seashells listen, an ear to the tide,
Whispering rumors of things they can't hide.
Nautilus raves in spirals so grand,
While dolphins giggle, waves on the sand.

Mysterious Murmurs of the Abyss

In the deep, where darkness writhes,
Eels play tag with the fish that thrives.
A sponge sings softly, runs out of breath,
While shrimp crack jokes about their own death.

The lanternfish flash their quirky light,
Winking at creatures all through the night.
Squids hide secrets in colors so bright,
While plankton laugh at their drifting plight.

Secrets Carried by the Current

The tide tales swirl in a playful breeze,
As sea cucumbers share some cheese.
Crabs hold meetings in their sandy keep,
While currents hum lullabies, deep and steep.

Starry skies mirror on waters blue,
Whales belt out tunes in a jazzy crew.
Coral reefs gossip about passing ships,
While anemones wave their floppy lips.

Unraveled Myths of the Ocean Floor

The crab in a tux, a sight so rare,
Dances with clams without a care.
Fish gossip about the mermaid's missed date,
While octopuses juggle, it's quite the fate.

Shells whisper secrets, they giggle and leer,
As starfish share tales of lost treasure near.
A pirate's old ghost with a parrot in tow,
Complains of the tide; it just won't go slow.

Elemental Secrets of the Blue

In deep blue waters, jokes float like foam,
A whale's got a knock-knock, just chills at home.
"Lettuce in there?" the dolphin did bark,
While fish share puns in the shimmering dark.

Mermaids with hair made of cheeses and spouts,
Tell tales of lost socks when they swim about.
And crabs throw a party, with shells as their hats,
While sea cucumbers dance, in their fancy spats.

A Symphony of Water's Whispers

The bubbles are giggling, a frothy delight,
As sea turtles bicker, who ate the last kite?
Lobsters in sandals, a fashion faux pas,
Sing off-key tunes that you won't hear, ha ha!

A clam with a drum and a fish on the flute,
Make music so odd, it's bound to dispute.
They laugh at the crabs trying hard to keep time,
While seaweed sways to the rhythm, sublime.

The Silent Ballad of the Waves

When waves take a break, you might hear a squeak,
A jellyfish giggles, its humor quite unique.
"Why don't we ever see the ocean's true heart?"
"Because it gets shy when it's playing its part!"

The parrotfish chuckles, "I once lost my hat,
Found it on a seal; he looked quite the brat!"
And lobsters convene for their monthly advice,
On how to escape from becoming fish fries.

Unseen Horizons of Untold Truths

Bubbles rise with silly tales,
Jellyfish whisper, in their veils.
Starfish grinning like they know,
Secrets of the tides that flow.

Seagulls gossip on the breeze,
Telling fish to just say cheese!
Turtles laughing in delight,
Swimming past the moonlit night.

Waters of Whispered Wishes

Mermaids sing in silly tones,
Trading seashells, not their phones.
Whales roll by with hearty chuckles,
Belly flops and playful huddles.

Crabs in tuxedos dance with flair,
Clapping claws, without a care.
Messages from finned friends swirl,
Like rubber ducks in a playful whirl.

Soothing Voices from the Abyss

Octopuses don their best hue,
Holding wise debates with sea otters, too.
Clownfish jest with painted grins,
Life's a joke where laughter spins.

Pufferfish puffing, what a sight!
Creating giggles, purely light.
Under waves, the humor flows,
In every splash, a mirthful dose.

Hushed Reflections of Deep Waters

Urchins whisper, knotty thoughts,
About their love for tangled knots.
Floating past with silly ease,
Their heartfelt laughter rides the breeze.

Drifting dreams in quiet glee,
Every ripple hides a spree.
Echoes of the deep, they say,
Make waves that dance the night away.

The Unheard Voice of the Tide

The tide whispers jokes to the rocks,
    They giggle and dance in their frock.

Crabs tell tales with their claws so spry,
    While fish just roll their eyes and sigh.

A jellyfish floats, a comedian's glee,
With tentacles wiggling, oh so carefree.

Seagulls caw jokes to the beach in delight,
As the sun sets, all share laughs through the night.

Salty Confessions of the Horizon

The horizon spills secrets with each wave,
    Snickered by shells that misbehave.

A starfish giggles, plays peek-a-boo,
    While dolphins share puns, just for a few.

The boats tell riddle, the wind plays along,
    Making the waves burst into song.

As tides tumble in, they wink and tease,
    Leaving us chuckling with a gentle breeze.

Beneath Moonlit Waters

Glowworms sparkle beneath the night,
    Fish wear sunglasses, oh what a sight!

    A crab in a top hat, a real show-off,
    Tells fish jokes that make them scoff.

The moon beams down, a spotlight so grand,
    Creatures gather, laughs in the sand.

All under the waves, where laughter shines,
    A comedy club where humor opines.

Conversations with the Wind and Waves

The waves chat with the wind, quite a pair,
    Trading giggles and splashes in the air.

    A wave quips, "I'm feeling quite bold!"
The wind replies, "You're a sight to behold!"

    They swap silly stories, they can't stop,
    While kites overhead do a funny flop.

    Together they howl, they dance, and sway,
    Making us chuckle as we watch their play.

The Depths Speak in Silence

Bubbles rise like tiny thoughts,
Fish gossip in their watery spots.
A crab with a hat, oh what a sight,
He dances in shadows, feeling just right.

A dolphin jokes, swirling with glee,
Telling tales to a turtle nearby, you see.
They chuckle at ships, so clueless and proud,
While sailors just wave, lost in the crowd.

Octopus wears glasses, reading a map,
Trying to find where the lost treasures hide, perhaps?
A clam with a wink, yes it's all in play,
In the silence of depths, they laugh all day.

So listen closely when you're by the shore,
For whispers of nonsense that we can't ignore.
The ocean is giggling, it's plain to perceive,
In the silence of waves, it's fun to believe.

Songs of the Sirens Unheard

Siren songs spill under the waves,
But they're just pranking sailors, being knaves.
"Come join us!" they croon, but it's all a jest,
Trading fish for snacks, they feast 'til they rest.

One mermaid wears flip-flops, cheeky and bold,
While flip-flapping fish dance, oh so uncontrolled.
They laugh at the captains who can't find their way,
Thinking they'll follow strange tunes that betray.

An octopus DJ spins vinyl with flair,
"Dance like no fish is watching!" fills the air.
With a swish of a tail and a glittering wink,
They throw a rave party, raising a drink!

Bubble-blowing seahorse joins the fun,
In a conch shell, they're having a run.
The ocean's a party, though no one can hear,
With laughter and music, they have no fear.

Shadows Beneath the Surface

In the twilight water, shadows dive and swirl,
A starfish wears sunglasses, a cool little pearl.
Fish flex their muscles, showing off for the crowd,
While a snail on a skateboard feels quite proud.

Crabs hold a contest, the best sideways walk,
Making a fuss, even turning to squawk.
Anemones giggle at the shrimp's funny shoes,
While shells gossip softly, sharing their views.

"Hey, where's my sombrero?" an anglerfish cries,
His buddies just chuckle with mischief in their eyes.
In the murky depths, where shadows play tricks,
The creatures of ocean enjoy their sweet mix.

So peep below, where the antics abound,
In the ocean's embrace, laughter is found.
Underwater merriment, no one can see,
Just remind them to keep it silly and free!

Unveiling the Ocean's Mystery

Peeking through waves, what secrets are masked?
Giant sea turtles, performing their tasks.
With hats made of kelp, they're stylishly bold,
While fishy fashion shows never grow old.

A treasure chest laughs, it's too heavy to lift,
Filled with old socks, it's a hilarious gift.
Even the barnacles throw in their vote,
For the weirdest finds keeping them afloat.

A whale cracks a joke, causing ripples to shake,
While the minnows giggle, their sides start to ache.
In a world of whimsy, they dance and they play,
Sharing witty tales at the break of the day.

So next time you wander by a sparkling bay,
Remember the laughter that's hidden away.
For beneath the blue, where the weird creatures roam,
The ocean's no secret, it's a big funny home!

Sagas of the Lost Voyage

On a ship made of dreams and a fondue pot,
The captain lost his map, didn't give it a thought.
We sailed past an island shaped like a shoe,
The locals were friendly—just a little askew.

A parrot with wisdom sat perched on my knee,
It squawked, "Where's the treasure? I'm thirsty for brie!"
We dug up the beach, just some shells and a shoe,
I think we'll need more luck, and some danke, it's true.

The mermaids were laughing, it seemed they all knew,
Of sandwiches hidden in whole coconuts, too.
On board, we danced jigs, took our naps on the mast,
But the snacks were all gone—our bright fortune blast!

So here we are stranded, with fish in a trance,
Finding humor in fables, and strange island dance.
With each wave that crashes, our spirits stay high,
As we chart a new course—it's a slice of the pie!

The Calm Before the Current

Oh, the water was still, like a sleepy old dog,
With bugs on the surface, and a winking fog.
A rubber duck army floated just fine,
I swear they were plotting to sip some good wine.

The sails flapped around like my granddad's toupee,
While I tried to convince fish to join our ballet.
They just swam away with a flick and a glide,
I guess they hate dancing—it's how they reside.

A jellyfish wore glasses, looked smart as could be,
Trying to read something—a novel? To me!
I asked what it said, they just bubbled and swayed,
And I'm pretty sure laughter was all that they made.

With nothing to catch, we colored the air,
With stories of pirates, and snacks they could share.
As the sun set low, we plotted our fate—
To seize that old rubber duck! Now that's first-rate!

Lingering Thoughts in Tide Pools

In a tide pool so small, I spotted a crab,
Who claimed to be wise, just a shade of a drab.
He told me of journeys beyond the great blue,
But all he could show me was gooey entrees too.

There were starfish debating the best forms of art,
Creating sand sculptures (with a rubbery heart).
They'd argue for hours with foam on their tips,
And a seagull kept swooping to snag all their quips.

A sea cucumber pondered how it gets to be fat,
While a clam whispered secrets about next week's chat.
With each wave that crashed, I giggled and laughed,
What creatures we are, oh, the world's a great craft!

As I turned to leave, all the critters waved,
With their peculiar ways, oh, the friends that I braved.
With salty goodbyes, their wisdom sunk low,
Yet my heart hummed with joy—what a curious show!

Depths of Uncelebrated Glory

In the depths of the brine, where the lost treasures rest,
A clam threw a party, it claimed it was best.
With wonky old floats and shrimp cocktails on hand,
It raved all night long in its washed-up sand land.

The octopus DJ spun kelp with great flair,
While the fish formed a conga—you wouldn't dare share!

I tried to join in but slipped on a scale,
And ended up dancing with a very round whale.

The sardines in tuxes looked quite out of place,
As they twisted and shouted, all wearing a face.
But amidst all the laughter and wiggly fun,
The sea snickered quietly, "This party's not done!"

As we swayed to the rhythm of bubbles and glee,
I realized some parties just couldn't be free.
Next time I'll bring snacks and a splash of brash cheer,
From the depths of the ocean, let's party all year!

Celestial Whispers of the Ocean

Bubbles giggle, secrets flow,
Fish wear hats, as currents blow.
Crabs dance sideways, a silly sight,
In the blue depths, all feels right.

Starfish gossip on the sand,
Telling tales of a friendly band.
Octopuses juggling shells in glee,
While turtles float, sipping green tea.

Seagulls squawk in comic tones,
Chasing the waves, stealing bones.
Waves wash in with a playful roar,
Splashing all high, like never before.

Mermaids snicker, flick their tails,
Crafting shells into funny jails.
The ocean laughs, a vibrant jest,
In every splash, it's feeling blessed.

Tranquil Conversations of the Waters

Fish in hats and suits of foam,
Chatting 'bout their ocean home.
A dolphin jokes, 'I swear I'm wise!'
While sea urchins roll their eyes.

Crabs complain, 'Why is it warm?'
One shrieks, 'I'm not a barnacle swarm!'
Seaweed sways with laughter, too,
In this watery world, all feels new.

Gentle waves give a cheeky wave,
Tickling shells, they misbehave.
Drifting boats with silly signs,
Riding high on sea's punchlines.

Stars above listen in delight,
As rain splashes with a giggly light.
Oh, what tales the waters spin,
In every splash, the fun begins!

Reflections of the Unseen

Under the surface, giggles lurk,
Puffers puff with a funny quirk.
A fish sings off-key, quite bold,
Contemplating silence, but never told.

Bubbles talk in whirls and loops,
Gather 'round the playful troops.
Crabby grins and clownfish cheers,
Chasing away all our fears.

Turtles pondering life's big quest,
Wonder if wearing shell's the best.
Anemones wave, 'We're here for fun!'
In this watery world, we're never done.

Ripples giggle, making a scene,
In watery whispers, they're so serene.
A dance of fishes, swirling round,
In their laughter, joy is found.

Murmurs of an Ancient Sea

Old barnacle tales get retold,
Where dolphins dive with hearts of gold.
Seashells giggle, pile high in stacks,
Conch shells shout, 'Hey, we've got facts!'

Waves that splash with a hearty swish,
Flip flops lost make a funny dish.
Starfish smile, with five-pointed zeal,
Their laughter echoed, oh what a reel!

Sand dollars trade silly quips,
As sea cucumbers do short flips.
Amongst the tales, the currents dance,
Creating joy with every chance.

Seagulls swoop and tease the waves,
In sunlit splendor, joy it saves.
The ancient sea whispers in jest,
With every wave, it feels so blessed.

Entities of the Underworld

Bubbles rise like secret laughs,
Underneath the ocean's path.
Crabs in tuxedos, do a dance,
While fish ponder their circumstance.

Mermaids giggle with a twist,
Chasing treasures, they can't resist.
Octopus plays cards with jesters,
While sea cucumbers host the fests.

Jellyfish float, lost in thought,
Wondering if they're ever caught.
A whale's the king of silly songs,
Singing loud as he sways along.

Eels are the pranksters, full of glee,
Telling tales of who's the fastest free.
"With all this water, let's break to eat!"
As they feast on a krill-sized treat.

Enigmas of the Salted Air

Seagulls squawk in honking glee,
Arguing over who's the bee.
A crab gives sideways looks of doubt,
While tides debate the best way out.

The wind steals hats, a crafty ploy,
Making beachgoers shriek in joy.
Sandcastles rise only to fall,
"Please don't eat me!" they seem to call.

A dolphin flips, the crowd is wild,
"Look at me!" he says, like a child.
A clownfish juggles shells with grace,
Though all the while, it's losing face.

With salty air comes unexpected fun,
Every day's a new pun to be spun.
So pack your beach bag, don't forget a laugh,
Life's an ocean, just take a splash!

Whispers Beneath the Waves

Under waves, whispers glide,
Creatures chat with ocean tide.
Starfish share their latest finds,
As squids squabble, "He's not kind!"

A grouper's gossip travels far,
"Did you see that shimmering star?"
Seahorses spin their yarns so bold,
Of adventures like tales of old.

A clam retorts, "You've got it wrong!
I've the voice, you're all just song!"
And shells chime in with crackling cheer,
While plankton dance, full of sheer glee here.

The whispers keep the ocean bright,
In this world where fish take flight.
With each bubble, laughter creeps,
As the ocean secrets joyfully leaps.

Ocean's Silent Secrets

Secrets float without a sound,
In tides where laughter is abound.
Anemones giggle in their dress,
As whispers carry, no need to stress.

Turtles tell tales that never end,
About the sharks who just pretend.
A dolphin snickers, "Bubbles are lit!"
As friends rejoice in the ocean's wit.

Crabs conspire with shells in tow,
"Let's prank the fish, put on a show!"
Seashells exchange their gleaming glances,
In the depths where the comical prances.

With every wave, there's humor shared,
In a world where no one's scared.
So let the ocean tickle your soul,
In the silent depths, joy takes a stroll.

Unwritten Tales at Water's Edge

Seashells gossip on the shore,
Crabs wearing hats, asking for more.
Wave after wave, tales they spin,
While starfish dance, wearing a grin.

A buoy beeps a silly song,
Floats laughing, 'Hey, you can't go wrong!'
Seagulls squawk in silly chats,
As dolphins tease the flapping bats.

Sandcastles rise, then take a dive,
With moats that secretly thrive.
Clams tell jokes, an oystercatcher chortles,
In this seaside land of playful portals.

Every splash is a giggle or two,
Fish flip-flop in their best debut.
Under the sun, shenanigans play,
At the edge where shimmers sway.

Under the Quiet Canopy of Water

Bubbles float like giggly balloons,
Fish wearing glasses hum silly tunes.
Corals nod, with colors so bright,
As octopuses hold a dance party tonight.

A floating log is a jaunty boat,
Filled with frogs, singing, and trying to float.
Turtles trade old jokes, so grand,
While seaweed tickles the clumsy sand.

Squids scribble messages in the sand,
Silly doodles made by a playful hand.
With every wave, laughter's afloat,
As crabs form a conga on their little boat.

Here under the waves, fun will not cease,
With fishy laughs and jellyfish peace.
Watch as they twirl, swirl, and glide,
In the quiet realm where secrets abide.

Serenade of Moonlit Reflections

The moon dips low, winking at me,
With waves that dance wild and free.
Frogs croon ballads in quirky tone,
As silhouettes shimmer, making it known.

The tide rolls in with a playful push,
And crickets chirp with a merry hush.
Starfish twirl, in twinkling delight,
While fish tell tales of their wild flight.

A humorous crab becomes a star,
Wearing a shell, saying, 'Look at my car!'
As dolphins leap, painting the night,
In this moonlit realm, what a sight!

Echoes of laughter rise with the swell,
Under the stars, where stories dwell.
Every ripple a punchline, fresh and bold,
In reflections of silver and shimmering gold.

Echoing Dreams of the Deep

Down in the depths, where the giggles reside,
Fishy comedians put on a slide.
Whales tell stories, grandiose and wide,
While minnows chase a runaway tide.

Eels are the noodles, swirling around,
Tickling the turtles who turn all around.
Sardines dance a jitterbug spree,
In a kaleidoscope world, so carefree.

Jellyfish bounce with a jelly-like jig,
Making everyone laugh with a jiggling dig.
Each wave carries whispers, jokes anew,
As the ocean smiles and splashes its hue.

Down here in blue, dreams spark and gleam,
With fish on a quest for the best ice cream.
What a funny world, deep out of sight,
Where every creature is full of delight!

Twilight's Reflections on the Waves

Twilight spills gold on the waves,
Fish wear tiny sunglasses, so brave.
Crabs dance tango on the shore,
They clap their claws, always wanting more.

Seagulls gossip with the breeze,
Telling tales of sun and tease.
Mermaids with laughter, a finned delight,
Throwing parties under the moonlight.

Starfish gather for a game of chess,
With shells as pieces, they're a real mess.
Octopuses juggle with style and flair,
While turtles talk about their hair.

So as the sky shifts shades of pink,
You can hear the waves begin to wink.
Nature's jesters in ocean's hall,
Making us laugh, one and all.

Luminous Secrets of the Dunes

Sandcastles tumble, oh what a sight,
Even the crabs think it's a fright.
Blowing winds play a tune of cheer,
While tumbleweeds pirouette near.

Dunes are pillows for sunbaked dreams,
Where lizards plot, or so it seems.
The shadows of cacti wear tiny crowns,
While the sun teases, giggling down.

Buried treasures kick up a fuss,
As crabs stage a heist, riding the bus.
Whispers of secrets shimmer and glide,
While geckos dance, their pride the guide.

At twilight's end, shadows blend,
As we ponder where pranks will extend.
The world's a joke, or so it seems,
As dunes reveal their nighttime themes.

Promises Written in Shells

Seashells whisper of love and cheese,
Their messages travel with ocean breeze.
Snails in tuxedos, oh what a sight,
Swaying together with all their might.

A conch shell holds gossip from the deep,
Of fishy romances that never sleep.
Starfish play matchmaker, what a twist,
Dreaming of partners in a salty mist.

Inside those shells, laughter resides,
Where ocean creatures go on joyrides.
Each whisper echoes a humorous tale,
Of jellybeans dancing at the coral trail.

So pick up a shell, give it a listen,
You might find surprises that make you glisten.
Promises linger in a salty swirl,
In the shell's hidden heart, laughter unfurls.

Language of the Drowning Stars

Stars sprinkle giggles on waves so bright,
Whispers of jokes dance into the night.
The moon chuckles, a silvery muse,
As dolphins perform with shoes of fuse.

Sardines sing in harmonious glee,
While shoals of fish join the lively spree.
Waves tickle shores with a playful tease,
As night unfolds like a party, with ease.

Bubbles rise like secrets untold,
Each one a portal to laughter bold.
The cosmos winks at this joyful show,
While crickets join in, stealing the glow.

When dawn approaches, the stars yawn wide,
Drifting back home, on the ocean's ride.
But in their wake, the laughter remains,
Echoing softly through sunlit lanes.

Limitless Blues of Untold Tales

In the depths where minnows dance,
A crab attempts a clumsy prance.
Whispers of fish with fins so bright,
Laughing at a sea snail's plight.

Turtles wear hats, they think it's cool,
While seahorses attend clown school.
Octopuses showing off their flair,
Dancing jigs in salty air.

Gulls squawk tales of days gone by,
While starfish just roll their eyes up high.
A dolphin sings, but it's off-key,
Still, everyone joins in with glee.

In waves they chuckle, splash, and spin,
A party where the fun won't thin.
With laughter bubbling up like foam,
Where every fish can call it home.

Currents of Quietude

A clam keeps secrets, oh so still,
While anemones wiggle with thrill.
The quiet tides carry funny sights,
Shy jellyfish in essence and lights.

Barnacles gossip on the old ship's hull,
While waves break patterns, ever so dull.
A seagull swoops down to steal a fry,
As crabs shake their claws, "Hey, that's our pie!"

Silent squids in a game of charades,
While eels wear wigs made of seaweeds' braids.
The ocean grins with a watery smile,
As it hides its quirks in every mile.

Serenity marked by a mischief's touch,
For who knew the calm could be so much?
In these quiet currents, humor flows,
With all of nature striking funny poses.

The Language of Lost Treasures

A scallop's pearl is worth a laugh,
For it thinks it's royalty by a giraffe.
Gold doubloons with a salty breeze,
Just hold stories through time's tease.

Mermaids trade secrets with a wink,
As barnacles nibble and pause to think.
A treasure map drawn in crayon bright,
Leads to the chest of a pirate's kite.

Old chests full of mismatched socks,
Sailor's dreams disguised as rocks.
Nautical nonsense we treasure here,
In the playful depths, we persevere.

Legends laugh beneath the waves,
While lighthearted whispers make new braves.
For each lost pearl and copper coin,
Hides a tale the tides will join.

Veils of the Distant Horizon

Sailboats chase clouds like kids at play,
While dolphins plot mischief, come what may.
Misty veils drape the horizon wide,
As seagulls scoff and rollercoaster ride.

In shadows of sunsets painted with cheer,
Fishermen tell tales we long to hear.
With flounders plotting their escape,
Caught in the nets, "Oh, what a landscape!"

A lighthouse flickers, "Who's there?" it beams,
While crabs orchestrate their goofy dreams.
With hiccuping waves, they spill their fun,
Beneath the glow of the setting sun.

As the stars peek through the sky's soft sweep,
Whales sing funny lullabies to sleep.
The horizon teases with a wink,
In the ocean's joy, we nod and think.

Whispers of the Deep

Beneath the waves, a fish did giggle,
It tickled a snail, who began to wiggle.
A crab in a top hat danced with glee,
While jellyfish swayed in a quirky spree.

The octopus boasted of ink so spry,
Said, "I make words that make the seagulls cry!"
But every creature just rolled their eyes,
For they knew his tales were funny lies.

A lobster proclaimed he'd found a pearl,
But it was just a shiny swirl.
Starfish chuckled, told a joke or two,
While the clams laughed hard, and the barnacles too.

So deep below where the sunlight fades,
There's humor hiding in oceanic shades.
With each splash and bubble, tales take flight,
In a world of laughter, they shine so bright.

Echoes Beneath the Waves

Listen close to the caverns so grand,
Where sea turtles meet and gently band.
A dolphin squealed, with joy it swirled,\nWhile sea cucumbers shared a strange world.

A fish pulled a prank, it nipped a toe,
"Oh dear!" cried the crab, "That's quite a show!"
The seashells snickered, clicked in delight,
As the flounder flipped, a comical sight.

Bubbles danced up like jokes on the rise,
With tickles and giggles beneath the skies.
Every splash held secrets, and every wave,
Had laughter tucked in, quite bold and brave.

So when you hear echoes beneath the foam,
Remember there's humor in their saltwater home.
In this underwater realm, fun does abound,
As creatures harmonize with joy all around.

Secrets in Tidal Currents

In swells and ripples, there's wit galore,
From the giggling plankton on the ocean floor.
A wise old turtle, shell full of wisdom,
Shared silly tales of jellyfish rhythm.

A clam told a story about a bad day,
How the sunburnt shrimp couldn't find their way.
Crabs laughed so hard they almost fell,
Echoes of laughter in the current swell.

Fish were trading jokes like shiny coins,
While the seaweed swayed to their funny groins.
Anemones tickled each curious face,
As sea stars shared a comical grace.

So heed the whispers of currents that play,
They dance with secrets, in a silly ballet.
When the tide comes in, forget your woes,
And dive with the humor that only it knows.

Currents of Silent Stories

In the depths where silliness ebbs and flows,
Silly fish schools wear mismatched clothes.
A shark with a bow tie and goofy smile,
Dreamt of becoming a surfer, just for a while.

The seahorse, a tiny knight in a vest,
Declared every tide was a chance for a jest.
"Why did the barnacle refuse to dance?"
"Too clingy!" it said, with a knowing glance.

The tides carried tales to the sands up high,
Of the starfish who learned to jump and fly.
With every wave that rolled ashore,
Was laughter hidden that begged for more.

So if you glance at the waves with a grin,
Remember the giggles swimming within.
For currents bring tales, both silly and sweet,
In the world's blue expanse, just tap your feet.

Riddles Hidden in Foam

Waves whisper secrets, laugh in delight,
Bubbles so cheeky, take off in flight.
Sandcastles tumble, like dreams in a rush,
Crabs dance around, in a mad little hush.

Seagulls are jesters, squawking their jest,
They snatch up our fries; it's all in their quest.
Fish flip and flop, in a splashy parade,
What's that fish saying? Oh, is it a trade?

In tides full of giggles, shellfish conspire,
With seaweed wigs, they look quite the liar.
Each tide brings laughter, as waves start to tease,
Do they ponder our snacks? Is it late for some cheese?

Jellyfish giggle, they jiggle and sway,
With stings made of silliness, leading us astray.
In this salty circus, oh, what a delight,
Nature's own comedy, both day and night.

Beneath the Roar, a Gentle Truth

The ocean's a storyteller, frothy and loud,
Yet whispers of wisdom hide in the crowd.
With shells that enchant and starfish with flair,
Is that Paul the starfish? With time to spare!

Sand dunes are pillows for dreams left behind,
Where seagulls plot mischief, so much unrefined.
Manatees giggle, they glide with a grin,
Or are they just waiting for snacks to drop in?

Dolphins in dialogue, spinning through blue,
They wink at each other or maybe at you.
The waves like a stage, with performers galore,
Jokes that are buried and truths we adore.

As nightfall descends, the tide starts to snore,
Each splash morphs to laughter, forever in core.
In foam-laden coves, the whispers grow strong,
The heart of the ocean sings its silly song.

Mysteries Cradled in Coral

Coral castles sparkle, a bright, bouncy play,
Where neon fish giggle and frolic away.
An octopus winks, with its eight arms in swing,
Is he plotting a prank? What chaos will bring?

Turtles in shells, like a slow-motion race,
Cheering each other with shells full of grace.
Lobsters hold bickering debates near a rock,
About who's the fastest or who's got the clock.

The ocean's a riddle of laughter and cheer,
With bubbles that pop like jokes in the air.
Barnacles huddle, whispering tales,
Of crabs with big boots and fish in high sails.

As the sun sets low, the colors ignite,
A splash of confetti, what a joyful sight!
In the coral's embrace, the mysteries thrive,
With humor and mischief—oh, how can we dive?

Whispers on the Windward Side

Tickling the shorelines, the breezes do sing,
In notes that go giggling, what joy do they bring?
Palm leaves are chuckling, swaying in mirth,
As if to announce that it's party time's birth.

Footprints in sand leave tales to be found,
Of summer shenanigans, laughter abound.
Starfish with smiles, like they know the good news,
Did you see the splash, or forget your own shoes?

The tide rolls in softly, an invitation so sly,
Let's build up some castles as seagulls all fly.
The horizon winks brightly, like secrets in flight,
This world is a playground, where day turns to night.

As moonlight embraces the waves with a laugh,
The ocean holds stories, with its own autograph.
So listen how it chuckles, as it tumbles and sways,
A symphony of humor in its infinite ways.

Driftwood Confessions

A stick with secrets, floating by,
It whispers tales of fishy lies.
A crab is laughing, pinching tight,
As gulls perform their aerial flight.

Old bottles bob with laughter inside,
Each wave's a joke, a playful ride.
The starfish chimes in, all aglow,
Sharing gossip of squid down below.

Shells hold memories, a clamshell's grin,
Confessions of clumsy fish who swim.
With every splash, a chuckle rises,
As the ocean's heart contemplates its prizes.

So driftwood dreams under moon's bright beam,
With laughter shared, it forms a team.
Each wave a punchline, oh what fun!
The ocean's humor has just begun!

Unmasked by the Tides

A lobster grooves in a sandy dance,
Waving claws like it's got a chance.
The seaweed sways, don't call it shy,
It's merely practicing for a tide-high fly.

Waves crash down with a giggling sound,
They whirl and twirl like they're spellbound.
A fish in disguise, a finned charade,
Making faces, unafraid.

A dolphin dives with a cheeky glee,
In a playful game of hide and seek.
Each splash reveals a secret smile,
As currents trick them all the while.

So now we see, as worlds collide,
The humor flows with the ebbing tide.
For every wave that comes and goes,
There's laughter hidden, it ebbs and glows.

The Unheard Symphony Beneath

Underneath the surface, a band does play,
Where bubbles whistle, and fish sway.
Clams tap their toes, in rhythm so sweet,
While sea urchins present a prickly beat.

A turtle hums a mellow tune,
As corals dance, they're over the moon.
With every flip, the flounder grins,
Making music from all their fins.

A sea cucumber strums a slime guitar,
While octopuses juggle from near and far.
Each wave carries notes of silly cheer,
An underwater concert, loud and clear!

So when you swim, don't just float,
Listen close to the aquatic quote.
For beneath the waves, it's quite a scene,
A hidden symphony that's wildly keen.

Blackened Reefs and Silent Dreams

In murky depths where shadows creep,
A clownfish dreams of a world so deep.
With blackened reefs, a party began,
Where even a crab can lead the band.

A sea slug slides in a colorful coat,
While sponges gossip and silly fables float.
Anemones wave, join the parade,
In a silent world, no need for charades.

Ghostly whispers in waters so dim,
Corals chuckle, sharing a whim.
Each flick of a fin writes tales in the sand,
With laughter carried by a friendly hand.

So if you wander where shadows play,
Remember the jests of the bold and the bray.
For in stillness, dreams often begin,
Where the ocean's humor shall never thin.

Beneath Shadows of Forgotten Shores

Upon the sands where secrets lie,
Crabs make plans as seagulls sigh.
They dance like no one's watching near,
While beach balls bounce and disappear.

With shells that whisper tales so grand,
Starfish gossip on the warm, wet sand.
The tide throws jokes that we can't hear,
Splashing laughter as waves draw near.

A flip-flop's fate, lost in the blue,
A sandcastle flagged—will it hold true?
But as the sun begins to fade,
The ocean chuckles, debts are paid.

So if you tread on beachy quests,
Beware of tides and their funny jest!
For every wave a wink could mean,
The shores hold humor, quite unseen.

Ephemeral Echoes of Time's Ocean

The tide comes in with laughter right,
Shells bounce back like jokes in flight.
A dolphin flips, a fish goes 'whoa!',
While crabs engage in a dance-off show.

Time drifts by in a rhythmic flow,
With beach umbrellas all in tow.
Seagulls squawk their punchline tune,
As waves create a swirling boon.

A jellyfish swims, all bob and weave,
It pulls faces as we believe.
The sun gives in to a watery laugh,
As mermaids call it their warm bath.

But stay awake, for waves might tease,
They'll tickle toes, if you're not at ease!
So ride the surf, let humor soar,
In nature's splash, we smile some more.

Fabled Currents of Silent Desires

Waves whisper tales on a salty breeze,
Where fish play chess with anemone tease.
Octopuses dress for a ball tonight,
While barnacles hold their shells so tight.

The seashells giggle, oh what a sight,
As sea turtles glide, all swoosh and light.
Crabby comedians crack jokes aloud,
Making fish laugh in the bustling crowd.

Sirens sing with a silly flair,
While tides tickle toes with a playful stare.
Each splash is a punchline, a watery jest,
And sea creatures know how to have the best.

From swaying kelp to the bright, bold gull,
The laughter echoes, making hearts full.
For in the deep where the humor runs,
The ocean's laughter never shuns!

Pathways of Water's Secrets

In hidden coves where shadows dance,
The fish wear hats and take a chance.
Mermaids chuckle with playful glee,
As waves spin tales just for thee.

The oceans swirl and tickle feet,
As dolphins plot their next big feat.
A ship's lost anchor sings a song,
Proclaiming loud that nothing's wrong.

Pufferfish puff with a bold, loud grin,
While sea cucumbers just sink in.
Each ripple hides a joke or two,
Waiting quietly for the likes of you.

So take a step and join this jest,
In watery realms where fun's the best!
For in the depths, the laughs are free,
And every splash just sings to me.

Palette of Silence Across the Sea

A sailor sat with bread in hand,
His boat was made of rubber bands.
He sighed and tossed a crusty slice,
The fish all giggled, oh so nice.

The waves did dance, a salty song,
As seagulls swooped, they whirled along.
The jellyfish wore hats with flair,
While crabs tapped toes without a care.

With every wave came whispers loud,
Why do the fish just laugh so proud?
In every splash, a joke was spun,
Between the tides, they all had fun.

A dolphin swooped with a wink and flip,
Surprising all with its funny quip.
The ocean's hum, a laugh on repeat,
In this vast blue, joy tastes so sweet.

The Unvoiced Voyage of the Winds

The wind had thoughts, but lost its voice,
It blew through trees without a choice.
A whispered word became a breeze,
Tickling cheeks with playful tease.

A parrot squawked, oh what a show,
Pretending it was in the know.
As kites flew high, they pranced and spun,
Chasing the laughter, chasing the sun.

The clouds conspired, all fluffy and white,
To play hide and seek from day to night.
With every gust, they made a scene,
Telling tales that could never glean.

The whispers floated, light and free,
On this wild, wacky spree.
With every gust and flying flap,
The winds just laughed and took a nap.

Enchanted Silence of the Underworld

Beneath the waves, where bubbles dance,
An octopus wore polka dots by chance.
He plotted schemes with tricky flair,
While clams played cards without a care.

The fish wore ties and had a ball,
They'd clap their fins in every hall.
With laughter bubbling like a drink,
The eels would giggle, "What do you think?"

In shadows deep, the seaweed swayed,
And sea horses strutted, unafraid.
Their ball was bright and full of cheer,
The deep was full of jokes, oh dear!

With bubbles popping all around,
The magic of the depths was found.
They whispered tales of silly fun,
In the underworld, they'd never run.

Distant Calls of the Deep Blue

From depths unknown, a strong voice yelled,
"We've got the best jokes!" everyone swelled.
The whales belted notes, comedic glee,
As minnows joined in, all chirpy and free.

With every splash, a tale was spun,
A crab recited a pun just for fun.
The starfish cheered, "You win a prize!"
While turtles laughed, rolling their eyes.

The jellybeans bubbled with glee and laughter,
For every word led to a raucous disaster.
The ocean echoed with giggles wide,
As every creature waved fishy pride.

When night fell soft upon blue cheeks,
The currents whispered as the ocean speaks.
With humor brewing beneath the waves,
The calls of the deep became hilarious faves.

Beneath the Surface of Thought

Bubbles dance with silly glee,
Fish wear hats, it's quite a spree.
Crabs have secret jokes to tell,
Behind their shells, they giggle well.

Waves whisper tales of fish and chips,
Seagulls steal snacks, do funny flips.
Inky squids with polka dot ties,
Rolling laughter under bright blue skies.

Seaweed sways, it's quite the sight,
Dancing like a ballerina, just right.
Starfish play cards with shells as foes,
Cheating with all their crafty throws.

Splashes of fun, a frothy song,
In the ocean, where all belong.
Each ripple sings, no tale too absurd,
In the deep, where laughs are stirred.

The Enigma Within the Waves

Crabby conundrums, riddles afloat,
Turtles in tutus, they twirl and gloat.
Octopuses juggle, showing off flair,
While sea snails drift without a care.

Waves contain whispers, oh so sly,
Mollusks laugh as they float by.
Algae pranks with a wobbly grin,
Tickling the toes of friends who swim.

Dolphins debate the silliest things,
Like who wore the best seaweed rings.
With a splash and a flip, they make their case,
Joyful chaos in this watery space.

Mermaids giggle in coral attire,
Swapping tales by the glowing fire.
Strange, sweet secrets weave through the tides,
As laughter echoes, the ocean confides.

Soundless Stories of the Current

The current carries wild, funny dreams,
Where jellyfish whirl in glittering beams.
With wiggly wigs and silly dances,
They float along, giving chance their glances.

Eels share whispers, a slippery chat,
While quirky clams wear hats that go splat!
The fishy gaggles laugh in delight,
In the ocean's embrace, everything feels right.

Waves crash softly with giggles and cheer,
Tales of clowns that swim without fear.
Amongst the whirlpools, fun does abound,
Joy forever in this watery ground.

A world beneath where laughter is king,
Each bubble rises, a curious thing.
With soundless stories, the current sways,
Floating lightly through all of our days.

The Lore of Water and Time

Oh, fishes tell tales as old as the tide,
With tales of adventure, where secrets abide.
Their fins all flutter, mischievous and spry,
In waters that shimmer like a wink in the eye.

The rocks have memories, wise and quirky,
Of ancient mariners and their tired jerky.
Waves clap with laughter, so merry and bright,
As bubbles and giggles take flight overnight.

Seals in sunglasses bask on warm stones,
Cracking up at their silliest tones.
With shells as their shields, they play hide and seek,
In the depths of the brine, the laughter's not meek.

As sunbeams dance on the frothy peaks,
Fishy philosophers share what they seek.
In waters embraced, there's joy that prevails,
With stories of humor spun in the gales.

The Language of Water's Embrace

Splashing waves wear silly hats,
Jellyfish dance like clumsy cats,
Gulls squawk jokes with feathered flair,
While seaweed winks in salty air.

Crabs in tuxedos strut with style,
Clams tell tales that make you smile,
Starfish play poker on the rocks,
Seahorses gawk at clockwork socks.

Octopuses juggle fishy dreams,
While dolphins plot their silly schemes,
Bubbles rise with giggles and sighs,
As salty secrets float and rise.

The tide delights in splashy fun,
Tickling toes 'til day is done,
Each wave a chuckle, a quirky rhyme,
In water's embrace, we lose all time.

Notes of a Crashing Tide

Waves crash down with a silly thud,
Whales hum tunes, and the water's a bud,
Seashells gossip, all twisted in glee,
As barnacles tap dance on the knee.

Fish wear sunglasses, feeling quite cool,
Seagulls recount each gullible fool,
Tides play tag with boats passing by,
While mermaids giggle in waves oh-so-sly.

Kelp sways like dancers in a line,
Pufferfish puff with comedic shine,
The ocean's choir sings off-key,
But who could resist their jubilee?

Echoes of laughter swirl in the foam,
Each ripple whispers, "Welcome home!"
In the water's embrace, joy's parade,
Where sunny antics are always displayed.

The Ocean's Cryptic Confessions

Sand tells secrets of lost flip-flops,
As jellybeans float and plop, plop, plops,
Fish in bowties juggle for fun,
While waves whisper tales under the sun.

Crashing surf gives a foamy smile,
Seagulls crack jokes with an airy style,
The tide writes stories in frothy ink,
Where sea cucumbers pause to think.

Clams with a joke or a funny pun,
Lobsters strut under the setting sun,
Coral reefs giggle in polka dot guise,
As dolphins wink with sparkling eyes.

With every wave, a chuckle breaks,
In the water's depths, humor awakes,
The fishes swim in a comedic whirl,
In ocean's depths, laughter's a pearl.

Heartbeats of Horizon's Edge

Waves crash like a ticklish tick,
Mermaids play leapfrog, what a trick!
Crabs march in line, wearing hats so wide,
While sprinkle fish slide down a slide.

The horizon giggles, stretching its face,
As turtles twirl in a slow-motion race,
Dolphins whistle tunes that make one sway,
In the watery world, they dance and play.

Sandcastles grumble, "Don't take my height!"
Seashells debate on who's a delight,
The tides play pranks with a splashy cheer,
Where giggles echo and fun is near.

At dusk, bubbles form stories untold,
As starfish share dreams of treasure and gold,
In waters that whisper and laugh with pride,
Life's a joke with a joyous tide.

www.ingramcontent.com/pod-product-compliance
Lightning Source LLC
Chambersburg PA
CBHW060147230426
43661CB00003B/599